# SPLENDOR

# SPLENDOR

Emily Bludworth de Barrios

www.h-ngm-nbks.com

FIRST H_NGM_N EDITION, March 2015

ISBN 978-0-9903082-2-5

Book design by Heidi Reszies Lewis
Cover illustration © Bri Hermanson

For a complete listing of titles, or for more on this book, visit:

www.h-ngm-nbks.com
www.h-ngm-n.com/splendor

# CONTENTS

and she was not sorry / 19

Be these omens from heaven or hell / 20

Some comfort it gave her / 21

she thought she heard a sigh. / 22

Cheered with this reflection, and hoping to find a friend / 23

they were soon wrapt from mortal eyes in a blaze of glory. / 24

and sometimes in thy prayers remember / 25

—but man was not born for perfect happiness! / 26

with a mixture of grace and humility / 29

and everything ready for beginning the divine / 30

He instantly set out for the wood that had been marked in his dream. / 31

re-echoed through that long labyrinth of darkness / 32

I was not always so great: / 33

the holy man remained absorbed in thought / 34

he felt returning love forcing itself into his eyes / 35

Thou knowest it has been the occupation of my life / 36

Yet her own situation could not help finding its place in her thoughts. / 37

Sure thou art not a mortal, but my guardian angel. On my knees let me thank— / 38

It is piety alone that can distinguish us from the dust from whence we sprung / 39

sure you do not suspect me of not feeling / 40

I know she longs to fold you in her arms, and assure you of her unalterable affection. / 42

with an air of firmness and authority / 43

using their gentle violence to stop and calm / 44

The dignity and patient firmness of Hippolita penetrated him with respect / 48

We are all reptiles, miserable, sinful creatures. / 49

The spectre marched sedately / 50

a thousand circumstances crowd on my mind / 51

until I have placed you in safety— / 52

For a considerable time she remained / 53

Follow me; dark and dismal as it is / 54

like that on the figure in black marble / 56

he beheld the plumage on the miraculous casque shaken in concert with the sounding of the brazen trumpet / 57

# SPLENDOR

May the saints guard thee

Your failure
feels treacherous inside you.

Treachery is when it turns out
that you were wrong about it all.

You lie smarting
in the bunk of your mind.

While the world lies disassembled
like a grievous injury
from which
you will never really recover.

There are effortless persons,
and you are not one of them.

Hush, hush.
Things will not be the same.

are the devils themselves in league against me?


It has been revealed to you
that you look upon things with an extraordinarily critical eye.

And this particular trait or flaw is
astonishing to you,

and how much we parade about with
that we don't in point of fact know about

though it's utterly obvious to every single body else
like if for instance you hosted a lagoon on your back

and in it a coral reef of delicate detail
with active and insect-sized divers and windsurfers

and shadows of moving carnivorous shapes
and schools of fishes and pill-sized turtles
scooping through a light-lit water

and this were common knowledge to the totality of your acquaintance,
and you come to find this out all of the sudden one day.

addressed herself to every saint in heaven, and inwardly implored their assistance.

Of course it is known that some people never grow up.

The stony need at the pit remains.

Poor souls.

To be bigger and older and draped
in knowledge and skin.

Having yet to have undergone
the great transformation.

and now with more serenity


I miss the old people
who are real grown ups

Who cared more about
farming than their interior lives

Make a mayonnaise sandwich and
fetch the water jar

Run it out to granddaddy over yonder

Old people more concerned with the correct way
of cultivating animals and plants

Than with plunging or plundering
their inner depths

Church was for panty hose and
Sunday songs

Let me fix you biscuits
and gravy

Come onto the back porch and
shell these peas with me

Old people strong as a cow or
a barrel full of dill

Playing dominoes in lamplight

The efficacy of regular work
smoothing away

Shards of inadequacy and disappointment
No space for a full evening of self-doubt

I'm going out to check the kittens in the barn

An awful silence reigned throughout those subterraneous regions

Just be yourself
is not such good advice.

In that it presumes the self is a defined entity
which one wishes to hide.

When the self is in fact
just loose.

One works to define a context
for one's life.

He sighed, and retired, but with eyes fixed on the gate.


It is possible
that one has extraordinary power
which one does not in actuality use.

So one believes.

Ambition loops in you
(lazy-headed, deep-spirited river).

You only wish to honor
your extraordinary power, what that might entail.

To work continually
is required.

In a best kind of self
is like how one may arrive.

I would pray to heaven to clear up your uncharitable
surmises

I always knew I would
marry a rich man.

You think I am joking.

I assure you I am not.

You wonder about my moral
core,

I sometimes and sometimes
don't have one.

I assure you that you are
better than me,

thinking your good
thoughts

which are impossible for
me to even conjure.

I can't even find examples
of them,

you and your good thoughts

appearing like milk and
green beans

on a supper table.

I always knew I would
marry a rich man

or else inherit a rich pot
of money,

which is actually true,

the family trust sits
obscurely in the bank

(but in my mental
framework it gains more and more concreteness

like a Caribbean island
growing more and more detailed

in the plane's window).

It assures freedom from a
certain kind of base suffering.

As a girl

I thought the richness
would be an inheritance from a long lost uncle

(I received this from a
book I read),

then from a prince
(another book),

then maybe a discovery
that I was the princess (another book),

then for a long time I knew
I would never receive wealth in this way.

It was not wealth I was
after but more like acclaim or arrival.

How beguiling is the sense
of unearned accomplishment.

That is something at which
one cannot fail.

I always knew I would
marry a rich man

and then I did.

Andres thinks it's gauche
to talk about assets and investments in front of strangers and
friends.

This money to me is a cave
of glittering orbs.

An assuredness of what I may
do in this life.

I live in a fantasy land
and nothing is this simple.

Of course Andres would
never use the word gauche.

He lives and things happen
as they are.

These scruples concurred to make the separation from her
husband appear less dreadful


Splendor, like a head with lines coming out.

To desire one very radiant thing.

I would like one thing to become clear,
then another.

Praise on you
who have your clear values to live for.

do not doubt my tenderness:


Kindness
is a plate of water carried on the head.

Whose water is flush with the brim,
and spills each time you are uncareful.

One must therefore be careful
all the time.

Easier to altogether dispense with the plate,
and act as you please.

Having basically spent your life perpetually dampened.

But still liking to be reminded
to try anyway to be careful and good.

uttered a deep sigh, and heaved its breast.


The touching will never be enough for him (the cat).
He is wanting new touching
on his face-whiskers, rump, back, and tail.
He regards me from the top of the fridge
like a lover all full with craving.
Like languishing from it, and not eating.
You know that kind of raw pain that feels so good
you want to become clean as bones,
pain like hunger, or a metaphorical burning.
Asteroid's just a cat though and isn't afflicted by that sort of thing.
I rock him in my arms, and we two-step across the kitchen.

were tempestuously agitated, and nodded thrice, as if
bowed by some invisible wearer


You almost love the things you own.
With a fitful, envious love

like you love the implied lives of fashion editorials.  Brief and single-
   minded,
they have gentle cheeks and throats.

So candy and persistent (your inner lunge for thing).

It sounds made-up,
a human desperate in love with thing.

I left a restless couch, and came to waste the irksome hours
with gazing on the fair approach of morning


        The purple hour.
Touch eyes on some
                purplish stuff.
Ambulatory.
Foamy snow.

Self-love is an odor
that takes getting used to.

Butter, mauve, minty snow.
Woolly mauve, velvet stones.

Impossible to be so
confident and knowing.

any increase of tenderness to me

All of the advertisements are like you you you.

Like this coffee travelled 1000 miles
to be the two perfect inches
of your espresso.

Or in one month
you will have more youthful-looking skin.

Which is another way of confirming
it is you who are central to this life.

leaving the amazed ladies thunderstruck with his words and
frantic deportment


You wake up ashamed.

Your errors spangle the ceiling,
what you might call the real you.

To be the best version of oneself
would be to live in pure silence,
i.e., never to speak, i.e., never to say these
wrong things.

It's very hard to do it.

You don't have to live in fear.
Your big mistakes have happened,
and will happen again.

and she was not sorry

Friends like accessories

As if to say       These were they and
These were they

A husband like an accessory
(One accomplishment)

A house A car Etc

One really great outfit you do not want to waste

A system of values twisted like a giant swirl
A swirl which reaches the sky like a tall staircase

To walk down or up the spiral of one's values
To walk with dignity       Very erect

Be these omens from heaven or hell


Another bad
type of emotion that remains below most silvery or polished
feelings

is a
great envy, which has the wistfulness of

a boat,
or a fine day that occurred at some time in the deep past.

When I
encounter it meaningfulness makes a sound or a feeling like
smoothness in water.

When one
feels low or envious there is the sound of the number zero.

It continues
in a circle and makes a noise like this:

## Some comfort it gave her

So many bad things have happened
that should not.

It's complicated, wanting to be
careful of the bereaved.

Bereavement almost sanctified
because it is so confined;

it actually cannot be
accessed from without.

Bringing rum, chocolates,
just murmurs of comfort.

But ultimately
not really helpful at all.

Empathy which one stands there holding
no place to put it.

she thought she heard a sigh.


The cars on the freeway make a gentle windy sound.
But because the cars are not the ocean
it is not really a gentle sound.
Instead it is a bitter sound.
At night the freeway's bitter wind drops into my dreams
where ornate houses stand beside the freeways.
The sound from the freeway drifts and covers them.
They darken with soot.
Only it is not soot, but something with a name that sounds more bitter.
The ocean is nearby.

Cheered with this reflection, and hoping to find a friend


One works to define a context
for one's life.

I lived in a house in the suburbs
it was like a manor.

I had no borders.

I ran on and on like a green expanse.

I who have been given so much it was not clear
where the world ended and I began.

It has been a process of choosing what to let in.

Nix.

It has been a process of practicing to be better.

At one's own direction
one must strive to be a particular self.

they were soon wrapt from mortal eyes in a blaze of glory.


As if you were a famous and celebrated painting.

Just hanging about
receiving praise.

It is an adolescent wish,
wanting to be praised for having done no thing.

When in reality
that would not make you feel accomplished.

You know it, in your intestines and your throat,
when you have contributed a genuinely good thing.

and sometimes in thy prayers remember


This is a Third World Country.
That has been agreed upon.

What a privilege to say so, how unlikeable.
(Also truthful.)

I was almost sure
it gets consistently easier,
to ignore how life for other people is hard.

(Say them salty, your favorite nuance words:
privilege, position of power, nuance.)

I know with my whole mind
I don't think about these things just right.

Why bring it up then.

Because I inherited a life
for which I am grateful.

(Tennis Club, this air,
very salty and physical.)

I am so far basically undamaged,
and therefore very lucky.

—but man was not born for perfect happiness!


In the suburbs there are white teeth
(crisp white frosty white snowcap

frozen fluorescent teeth)
Poorer people have more realistic teeth

Sometimes much more beautiful
(wide toothed gapped smile like a blow to the guts)

Sometimes less so
(a curled fist of teeth in a modest and apologetic mouth)

To be modest and apologetic makes one more loveable,
especially when the teeth are like a claw of a hand

Sometimes there is a single tooth which is way too forward,
or one that hangs in the shadows (a shadow tooth)

Or a dragon tooth pointing the way to righteousness
Also teeth which are totally the wrong shape

Also the pharaohs lying on slabs
doused with gold and inlaid turquoise

and eyes fashioned of deliquescent contours
in a room of gold chairs and steady oxen

and stars on the ceiling and teeth ground down in the mouth
from a lifetime of minute grains of sand

It is a terrific mouth of pain

Lapus lazuli, gold, honey, sex
and our delicate delicate delicate delicate teeth

with a mixture of grace and humility


Let us have a brief period of silence


During which time
you will think about nothing
and you will have the qualities of a silver coin

A period of silence
is a column with a hole at the top and a hole underneath

The second period of silence commences now


meaningless
a hole

and everything ready for beginning the divine


To each a parent or parents,
to whom one is born or given.

The mother or father
a plainly separate person

with his or her private ambitions
which cannot be perceived completely from without.

It is mysterious and startling,
how the parent is also
the important one of his or her particular epic.

And has all these concealments or isolated spaces
which occur in the thinking mind of a life,

and which are basically secluded
from others and from other points in time.

He instantly set out for the wood that had been marked in his dream.


The cat sits in the chair.
Night sits in the chair.
The apartment is full of things that don't move.
I'm just now interested in the way Asteroid
works his way towards sleep.
A ponderous slitting of the eyes.
The head which wobbles.
I shift and he opens back up.
Now like a pile of sand nodding off.
I could never be a pile of sand like that.
To be human is to think and do.
I must always be acting upon.
Through doing
I am the long art project of my life.

re-echoed through that long labyrinth of darkness


I had a dream that I was a baby writing a poem
and it was going smoothly or perfectly
and it was a page long or more and then I woke up
and now it's like
when the lights come up to show that the club closes
and we suddenly have faces
(made of shadows and flaws) again
and I feel minorly ashamed.
Babies don't write poems, and if they did
what would they be about?
Breasts, being held, warmth, coldness,
sleep, coughing. How when crying
your face is possessed by movement
tip to tip. Coming to terms with being alone.
Mother. Father. After the long hours.
Being so much smaller. A room moving
past you. The velvetiness of yourself
struggling in bedding, and socks.

I was not always so great:


Asteroid is always stretching the shit out of himself.
I could say a lot about Asteroid's habits, tendencies, etc,
but I'm not sure how interesting they'd be to you.
Each cat is exactly different.
It's not true that all cats are the same.
Asteroid's always trying to sip my glass, for example.
He's always winking his left eye.
His back knees almost touch like a girl who can't dance
and knows it
but longs with desperate love like a long white wishbone poking
   through her heart
that Cody Thomas will approach her seriously,
during Whitney Houston's *I Will Always Love You*.

the holy man remained absorbed in thought


Smooth as old rocks.
Warm stones.

                              Ocean glass,
or cliff made of glassy rock.

Like sitting inside a circle
                the flavor of gold,

beach-mind washes out and in.

*ugh*

he felt returning love forcing itself into his eyes


In Cairo the sounds from the street
jump or drift or push or dart up from the street

through the open doors onto the balcony
and they are arable sounds

(of men talking and boys shouting and horns tooting
and the call to prayer and a million sounds made by objects or people

moving, that you would not sift and distinguish upon hearing)
and you cannot help but feel wealthy or young-skinned

in the arid almost cool air-moving-through the various open
    windows and doors
of the apartment, all tiled and robed

at the helm of morning
also again you are the luxury one, how lucky

you have been among the Earth

Thou knowest it has been the occupation of my life

His interior (Granddaddy's) was pale blue.

As a herd of elephants
will stop moving completely and listen,
he would sit up within himself
even while doing a useful thing.

Just like a quiet cornflower,
quietly doing.

He was that kind of man
having a world inside to retire to.

Yet her own situation could not help finding its place in her thoughts.


Like a backpack, minuscule burdens
you carry around with you.

Which is okay generally,
these lacerations of the day.

It's more like an effort at love (to embrace the day, errors, etc).

To be doing your best
amid different shapes of lacerations.

The minor degradations are a modest sacrifice
to be a solid and a thinking and a living one.
You can take more of it.

Sure thou art not a mortal, but my guardian angel. On my knees let me thank—


As when a kitten chooses to make for its bed
your warm torso
and you feel very chosen.

It is hoped that
I am and continue to be a worthy participant.

To be loveable isn't to be good
but to be consistently going for it.

I.e. to habitually make one's life.

It is piety alone that can distinguish us from the dust from
whence we sprung


Another thing I never understood
was how and why some people

move through life like glittering scales
and others shrink and slip inside their skins.

And then you don't know which of the two
you are:
                    the shimmering one
or the mottled dish sponge afraid to speak

lest your words betray your confusion.
To continuously break and to continuously move forward.
Small- and medium-sized problems you find

in your path throughout your day like islands
you arrive at

in which to be always ascertaining your worth.

sure you do not suspect me of not feeling


Every place has admirable things in it.

In Bolivia two admirable things
are toborochis and the pretty yellow juice of maracuyá.

Also green (like jewels) sauce for steak.

Also things you can't see,
i.e., societal networks I can't or can barely perceive
(lines come together at various points).

In a new place like this
sometimes there is that experience
where you suddenly or briefly

or for a sustained period don't know what kind of person you are
(what your values, what your way of being).

Like my general expectation of being
pleased all the time

by which I mean to ambulate throughout
another's home as if it were a restaurant erected in my honor.

How I thought *Tico's house is
poorly decorated*

instead of
*This is where a family lives.*

These bouts of wrong thoughts;
it is my culture or it is my mind.

To be so at a remove
as to feel particularly cold sometimes here in a new place.

I know she longs to fold you in her arms, and assure you of her unalterable affection.

To have felt total love.

To have been totally in love.

One feels that one does not deserve.

To have been the improbable thing.

One wonders, can one remain so.

It did happen.

I was someone's discovered and improbable thing.

with an air of firmness and authority


I would be a mother
not knowing what it means.

I would be a mother
knowing nothing of what it means.

I would lift the mantle the yoke
put on the clothing of a new selfhood.

I would go where I have
not been.

To be celebratory and gorgeous.

And thwarting mine own ambitions.

It is a good moment to be so ignorant.

using their gentle violence to stop and calm


Now that we are trying to get
pregnant

A zygote continuously divides in
my abdomen

Inside my body it is another
universe

Etc etc it is very dark

Asteroid is also another universe

He has six nipples and will never
have kids

Though he would make a good
mother

And would be soothed I know

By six plump kittens suckling his
belly

And kneading it with miniature paws

He practices this laying on his
side with eyes half closed

And has the gruff and fixed attitude
of a mother

Now that we are trying to get
pregnant

Now it is a time in life
where one gets very

Superstitious with words and
thoughts

Like as if each could jinx
but I am like as if stepping into water

Windy leaves wind chimes toads
at night

Something very tranquil

Science is happening inside my
body

And I'm so casual

Like someone who never worries
about nothing

Not the stove, not zygotes

Just taking a walk at dusk around
the block

And making sure the dogs have
water

Becoming not so important

Maybe

Now that we are trying to get
pregnant

I
embark upon the misty path

One mythic brave humble hero

Feeling his way throughout
the world

I am sifting my values

As if to keep them in a
vault

Or articulate them in an
irrefutable way

Like a math formula that's true
for all the situations

A rock among variables

A rock among the hard quick
water

The most important thing in my
life is _____.

The dignity and patient firmness of Hippolita penetrated
him with respect

Tacit understanding is the new black.

There is no new "having a cow."

From now on
you be calm beneath the sky.

You be
getting stronger every day.

We are all reptiles, miserable, sinful creatures.


To be perfect and beyond reproach.

How like a saint. How better.

Of course however it will never be
(never neither being perfect nor beyond reproach).

It is therefore necessary
to dissolve the knowledge of your failures.

So that one may step forward.

Into the odor of one's life.

The spectre marched sedately

Ultrasound uses many technologies,
e.g., a wand, a screen, a keyboard.

With the wand many details can be seen.
The fetal pole like a balloon appearing not to be doing much only
floating low to the yolk sac wall.

But in actuality it is doing the job of growing all the time.

Getting somehow consistently detailed, and bigger.

So that it may
enter the bright world.

As a pilgrim sets out,
filled of confidence and anticipation.

So one hopes.

a thousand circumstances crowd on my mind


One chooses to believe all will be best.
It is crucial to do so.

Else one will be consumed.

It is insanity to conjure up fatalities or bad luck.

To think think think on all the bad.

How obvious
that that is no kind of life.

until I have placed you in safety—


Death being an irrevocable no.

The point at which progression stops.

But is not yet totally over.

Still having yet to pass the blood and tissue.

For a considerable time she remained

When the fetus
died it died I left it in that day

There was no baby
I put away my preparations

Something was
wrong with it it died

Putting away
the celebrations

## Follow me; dark and dismal as it is

I am five foot five
Female

I have curvy hair

It is the color of
A polished penny

I am special
In the way that you are special

Which is to say
Not very special

Except in the sense that
We are a particular identity

Deciding and thinking
Many several particular things

Your special moments
Are occurring now

Your special thoughts are
Occurring now and continuously

But are so wispy and curve-shaped
Intelligence is so wispy and practically barely-there

Miraculous each time it occurs the sentence
Spilling out your teeth you deserve

More of an applause or a rest for having
Made it thus far for having

Occurred thusly

like that on the figure in black marble


nobody wants the sadness.

nobody wants the sadness
unless it is like their sadness.

and then it is highly desirable,
especially if it is illuminating.

i.e., if it is a mirror to your own sadness,
mirrors reflecting mirrors into a long silver hallway

in which one walks.
sadness told in a delicate way
can be described as exquisite, poignant, or sometimes nostalgic.

sadness which is like complaining
is a usually rotten type of sadness.

framing is of the utmost importance.

to put a happiest frame
around the sad thing.

he beheld the plumage on the miraculous casque shaken in
concert with the sounding of the brazen trumpet


At that time
anxiety was in you like a scribble.

An oblivion-scribble
like a big piece of Abstract Expressionism
where your thinking brain was supposed to be.

That was like nothing.
It was a big waste.

One must decide to be different
if one wishes to be different from what one is.

You with your list of worries
smoldering.

Might as well
say goodbye to the realistic world.

I! my Lord!


It has been a life of striving.

To what end one knows not.

Having been wanting to have been
articulate good etc.

Your ideal self has always been
lurking.

Somewhere
the ideal self is sudden and kind.

—would I were well out of this castle.


One thing I would like
is to be different.

One thing I would like is to be grown.

The day is horrid.
Or hurried.

Children or adults continue to require
patience and kindness.

The kindness-source
wobbles.

You strive to get better than you are.

I.e., like a totally grown woman.

With a dish or jar on your head
filled with kindness water.

To be all the time like that
walking tall.

recovered a little from the tempest of mind into which so
many strange events had thrown him


When the bad thing really happens
you have to figure out a way to decide
that it is not actually bad.

You call it terrible beauty.
Name the jagged mass a learning experience
in which the exquisite growth of the faceted story of your life occurs.
Like the difference between a whole tree and a blasted tree
or a tree marred by monstrous growths.

In your years
you must have done this a few thousand times,
when you felt the full weight
of the genuinely bad thing.

How comforting it is.
You do it again and again.

After continuing silent for some time


All the dead
Surge in a crowd

On the other side of time

Each having collected
His or her stunning end

They beseech you to accomplish 100,000 tasks

One of which is
Think spectacular thoughts
Thereafter to speak spectacular things

If heaven has selected me for thy deliverer, it will
accomplish its work

I have never had a
desire to be so

very famous
except when I was

a girl

I suspected
(as you did also)

that I would be told one day
without warning that

I was in fact a
princess who had

been misplaced
I felt

special and I wanted
an external proof

something irrefutable

I imagine and then I
believe that everyone

feels this way special
and irrefutable and

seeking proof it's not
reproachable behavior

it's as a matter of fact true you are
special and in all this

millennia this is your
one time to occur

the princess of time is

here the unique one having
arrived to bestow upon us

her royal graceful presence
that is you

The evening being far advanced, the banquet concluded.


I feel shame in my skeleton
when I waste my life.

To be totally energetic
is a quality I covet.

As if one could use one's life.

the company were dispersed their several ways

I appear.
Asteroid appears.
Andres appears.
Pork chops, spinach, and rice appear.
Sunday morning disappears.
Asteroid sleeps on his side like a woman who models for a painter.
Andres disappears.
I appear or remain in the dining room alone.
A tremendous change is occurring all the time.
I am saturated with time.
I am heavy with it all the time.
I haul it like an appetite or a stomach.
I miss it when it goes.

Yonder behind that forest to the east

As a big cat drags the
corpse of a killed thing

Asteroid carries his
mouse-on-a-stick.

The stick from the
mouse-on-a-stick trailing a hollow, pencil sound.

Padding through the forest
of his life

snarls of pain or alarm
encounter him.

To which he reacts with
great energy,

like a splat taking
action.

Blaring a solution where
none did exist.

Like a totally efficient
professional.

After which he takes
refreshment

(grooming, napping, etc).

Becoming curled up, small,
or sometimes almost flat.

Such a tired thing that
lives.

I will remember you in my orisons, and I will pray for
blessings on your gracious self


I like I love I like I love I like I love.

After a while
the important words have no smell.

No "silky in your hand."
No all-the-windows-open.

No teeth-over-olive's-pit.

opening the window gently herself


And suddenly the snow piles are gone.
It's blue and windy as if to say
I am still here.

Recipient of the long gift.

April is for collecting pieces of the morning.

Like for instance to be really languorous.
A thing made of air and pining.

in a cold morning or a damp evening

If days were an item to be wrapt and kept.

One feels like one could, if given the opportunity,
say something really wise.

As if there are some words so powerful
one would keep them in a box.
Or locket. With hair.

My hair after I die
will be some kind of flag.

Debilitating after some time.

Reach me my beads; we will say a prayer, and then speak

I get scary
thinking about my coming life.

All the different ways to fail
or be failed.

No one can deny
how anxiety sits and looks into your face.

Desolation
has occurred and occurs daily in Earth.

Amazing to find
one has passed safely through it.

## If thou art of mortal mould

Wanting
always to be your young wife

I'll
die and get purple and black

Therefore
I am wanting to make

death
more like a story

A
story is a thrilling thing

to
hear or be inside of

Orpheus
torn apart by maenads

sounds
clean practically

A
story is capable

of
cleaning things up

Wanting
always to be your young wife

I'll
die and get purple and black

A
story so dark

it
ends like this

                So long

You
die       Me too

Imagining
a funereal bier

burning
on water at night

Glaze
of light on water

It
is an orange and glossy celebration

I
would love it

if
each death were a glorious death

with
a glossy celebration

Instead
of so little-seeming

(60
folks milling about on Berber carpet at the Jeter Memorial Funeral Home)

At
least the entire success of the dead

is
a glorious skyscraper we live inside

To
live among the technology and materials of the dead

Their
many contributions

jingling
from the sky

Wanting
always to be your young wife

I'll
die and get purple and black

I'll
fall apart like a cobweb

and
before that I'll break

probably

All
the dead skeletons

dancing
in the Earth

wishing
us well

infants
that we are

flying
across the sky

in
silver tubes worrying

With
a crooked list of priorities

You
must needs

arrange
your priorities

Continue
to work

Your
integrity securely pinned about you

Gather
the sleepy puppy

of
your husband

Get
your skin-to-skin contact

while
you're able

# INDEX OF FIRST LINES

## ACKNOWLEDGEMENTS

The titles of these poems come from Horace Walpole's 1764 novel *The Castle of Otranto*.

Thank you to the editors of the following journals, where some of these poems initially appeared:

*B O D Y*, *Clinic*, *H_NGM_N*, *The Hollins Critic*, *ILK*, *Matter*, *The Pinch*, *Route Nine*, *SPECS*, *Tender*, and *UCity Review*.

Thank you to Emily Pettit and Guy Pettit of *Factory Hollow Press*, which published a chapbook containing a number of these poems.

I am grateful to Andres Barrios, Dara Wier, Violetta Beckerman, Lina Mounzer, Phyllis Bludworth, Sarah Hoffman, and Paloma Garner for their guidance and support. Thanks also to Bri Hermanson for creating the cover illustration and Heidi Reszies Lewis for designing the layout. Thank you to Nate Pritts for bringing this book into print.

Emily Bludworth de Barrios is a poet. *Splendor* is her first full-length book of poems. She lives in Houston.

**H_NGM_N** was founded in the fall of 2001. Originally a mimeographed and side-stapled poetry 'zine, **H_NGM_N** transitioned to the current online format for the journal in 2004.

**H_NGM_N Books** was formed in 2010 and releases 3–5 titles per year—most of which are selected through our Annual Open Reading period (November–March).

**H_NGM_N** flourishes at the nexus of old tech and new: dittos and screens, human hearts and digital speed.

**H_NGM_N** is a way of life, a type of attention.

www.h-ngm-nbks.com

18623122R00064

Made in the USA
Middletown, DE
13 March 2015